About this book…

The question, 'Where do babies come from?' cannot be answered simply with a scientific explanation. God, love, marriage and families must be included if children are to get a true picture of themselves and their origins.

That's why this book is careful to show the wonderful facts of life in their proper human context, making sure that God is given due credit for inventing the whole idea in the first place!

The book is intended principally for parents and children to read together, but teachers may well find it helpful too. In preparing it we have drawn from our experience of answering the questions our own children have asked. We hope it will help you talk about what can be a complicated and potentially embarrassing subject.

As you will see, we have treated the details frankly since children like to know the whole story. Naturally, you should feel free to use this book in the way that best suits your child's level of understanding. You may feel happier leaving bits out to explain later. And you can, of course, add any extra qualifications or explanations you think necessary.

We hope you and your children will enjoy exploring this exciting part of God's world together.

Malcolm and Meryl Doney

First published in the UK by
Marshall Pickering Holdings Ltd, 3 Beggarwood Lane, Basingstoke, Hants, RG23 7LP

© Marshall Morgan & Scott Publications Ltd, 1987
Text © Malcolm and Meryl Doney, 1987
Illustrations © Nick Butterworth and Mick Inkpen, 1987

British Library Cataloguing in Publication Data
Doney, Malcolm
Who made me?
1. Human reproduction—Juvenile literature
I. Title II. Doney, Meryl III. Butterworth, Nick IV. Inkpen, Mick
612'.6   QP251.5

ISBN 0 551 014768 (UK)

Printed in Italy

WHO MADE ME?

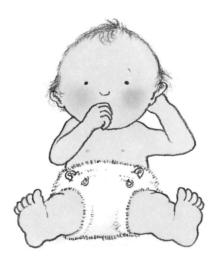

Text by Malcolm and Meryl Doney
Illustrated by Nick Butterworth and Mick Inkpen

Marshall Pickering

Have you ever wondered if there's anyone else just like you?

Well there isn't! There's only one you. No one else in the whole world is exactly like you. Not even if you're a twin.

But how did you come to be you? Who made you? What were you like before you were a baby?

It's an amazing story. It begins with Mum, Dad and God.

In the very beginning, God made the world and everything in it, trees, plants, animals and people.

So does that mean he made you?

The answer is, 'yes he did' and 'no he didn't'!

He certainly invented people. He designed us and made that amazing invisible power inside we call life.
It's what makes us living people,
not just robots.

But he didn't actually make you. He gave that important and exciting job to Mum and Dad.

When he first made people, God decided there would be two different kinds. Men and women. Between them he gave them the ability to make new people and bring them into the world. A whole family of them if they wanted.

This is how it works. Men and women, boys and girls are the same in lots of ways. But, as you know, their bodies are different. You can see this best when they've got no clothes on.

Boys have a dangly thing between their legs. Different families call it different names, like a willie or a winkle. Underneath it, there is a small sack made out of skin with what feels like two balls in it. (Most people actually call them balls!)

These have strange-sounding proper names. The willie is really called a penis, and the balls are called testicles.

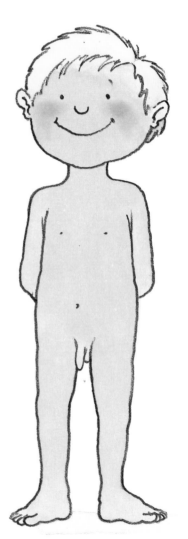

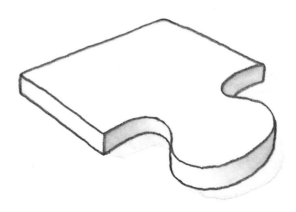

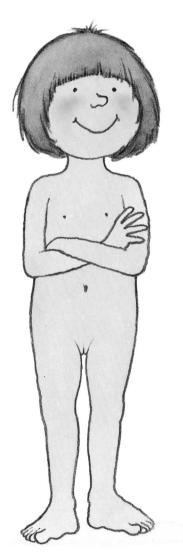

Girls have a mound that looks something like a little bottom between their legs, and it has an opening in the middle.

We can't think of a friendly name for it, so we just use its proper name. It's called the vagina.

These parts of our bodies are a bit like two pieces of a jigsaw puzzle. We're made that way so that later mums and dads will fit together, as you will see in a moment.

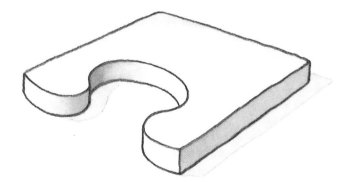

As you grow up, your body gets ready to become a mum or a dad.

A boy's penis grows bigger and hair grows around it.

As boys get older they grow hair in other places too. Grown-up men can grow beards, though often they prefer to shave them off. Some men have hair on their chests and arms and even on the backs of their hands!

Girls grow hair round their vaginas too. But something else happens as well. Their hips become wider so that there will be room for a baby to grow inside their tummies.

Soft mounds grow on their chests where those small round circles called nipples are. We call them breasts. One day they will be able to hold milk to feed a baby.

By the time a boy has become a man, his testicles are able to grow millions of tiny things inside called sperm. They are too small to see, but they look a bit like tadpoles.

Each one of these little things carries life, like a seed. But they're not like flower seeds; they won't grow into babies on their own. They can only do half the job.

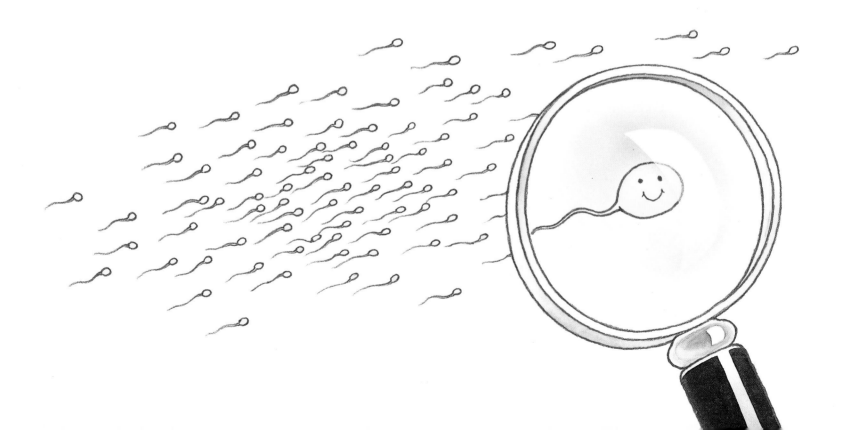

By the time a girl becomes a woman, there is enough space inside her tummy for two important things.

The first is a kind of room where the baby can grow before it is born. It's called a womb.

The second is a place where she keeps her eggs. (Yes, people have eggs too – not just chickens!) These eggs are soft and have life in them, just like the man's sperm. They are tiny too – you could fit quite a few on the head of a pin! The egg is the other half needed to make a baby person.

So, before a baby is made, the two halves – the sperm and the egg – have got to come together.

That's where the two pieces of the jigsaw come in.

God's idea for making babies was that a man and a woman should love one another so much that they want to spend the rest of their lives together. That's why people get married.

He invented them a special game to play together, to show just how much they love each other. We call it 'making love', and it's just about the best game mums and dads can play.

This is what happens. They start by kissing and cuddling. This is great fun, and mums and dads can get quite excited, so excited that the dad's penis becomes stiff, ready for the important bit that comes next.

They like to get their bodies as close as they can. The closest they can possibly get is when the man slides his penis into the woman's vagina.

Now the man and woman are sort of joined together, like two pieces of a jigsaw puzzle.

Mums and dads like being fitted together very much. They wriggle about like this for some time. Eventually they both feel so excited they could burst. A delicious shiver runs all over their bodies, and at the same moment the man's penis pumps up the sperm like a fountain.

They pour inside the woman, and swim to where the egg is waiting.

Thousands of sperm gather round the egg and the first one to push his way into the egg is the winner!

When the sperm and the egg meet, a wonderful thing happens. The two join together and become one. This is the moment when the new baby begins. We call it being conceived.

After all the excitement of making love, the man and the woman feel a bit tired. Like any game, it takes quite a lot of energy.

Meanwhile, inside the mum's tummy, the egg finds a cosy place where it can rest and grow into a baby.

The baby needs food to help with all this growing. But it's not ready for chips yet! Instead, it shares its mum's food through a special tube that goes between the side of the womb and the baby's belly button.

That's why you have a belly button. It's real name is a 'navel', and its where your food used to go in!

At first, no one can tell that the baby's there, but soon Mum can feel it moving around. Sometimes the baby kicks so hard, she thinks it's playing football!

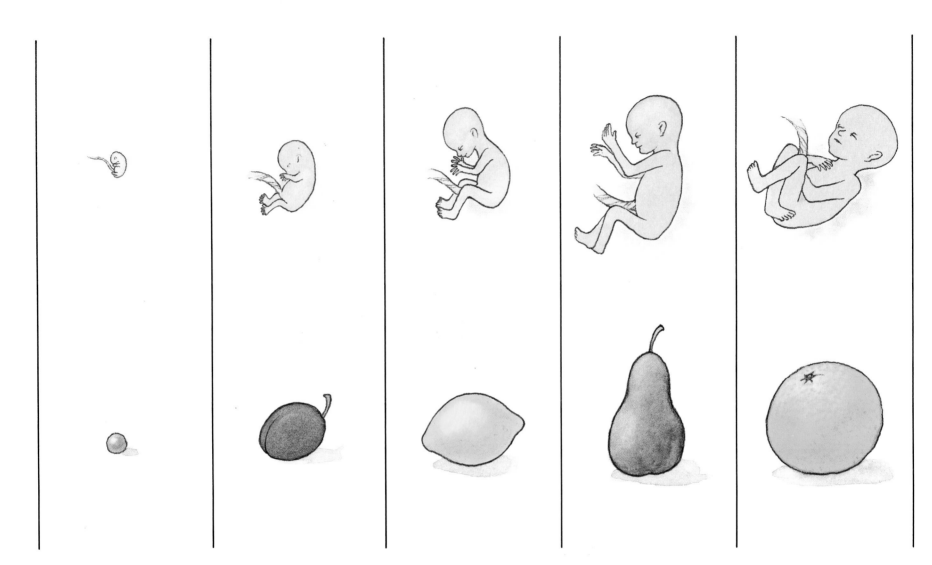

Here you can see how a baby grows in the womb,
month by month.

It's amazing to think that in nine months it can grow from a tiny egg, smaller than a pinhead, into a living, laughing, crying human being!

At last, the great day comes when the baby is due to be born. How does he get out? He can't walk!

Once again, Mum's body is ready to help. There is a special tube, between her womb and the opening between her legs. Her womb has its own strong muscles, and these get ready to squeeze the baby along the tube and out. This squeezing gives the mum a pain in her tummy. As soon as she feels this pain, she knows that the baby is coming.

It's very hard work for the mum,
to squeeze and push her baby down the narrow tube. She is
helped by doctors, nurses and someone called a midwife, who's
an expert at helping babies come out. And, of course, Dad's
usually there because it's just as much his baby as Mum's.

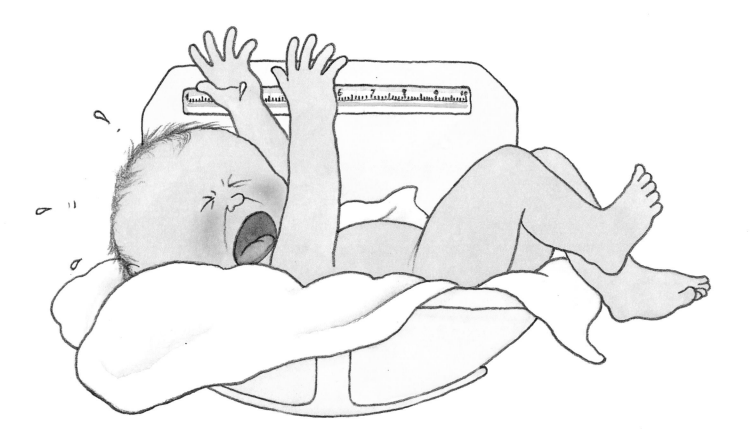

It can take a long time, but finally the baby is squeezed out, head first.

Being born is hard work for the baby, too. They often look cross, red in the face and rather squashed!

After so long in a nice warm dark place, the outside world is rather a shock. They usually open their mouths and…YELL!

Mum and Dad sometimes cry a bit too
because they're so happy!

Not only that, God is happy as well. Remember, he has
known you since you were just a sperm and an egg! He's glad
you're alive and he loves you very much.

So here you are, a special, living, growing person, made in this marvellous way by Mum and Dad.

And God made you too. Because mums and dads and babies were all his idea in the first place!

The ~~end~~ beginning!